SECR

DEVON

– Places to visit on Dartmoor and in the South Hams –

CONTENTS

INTRODUCTION

Researching and writing this book has been a memorable experience. Dartmoor and the South Hams are areas of Devon I have known and loved for a long time but having a reason to explore and discover new places and then write about them has been fascinating and hugely enjoyable.

The locations I have chosen all have a back story. Something that sets them apart in different ways. It could be because of what they tell us about the past, their setting or the legends that surround them. Each is special and, whilst some are easily accessible, others are a little more demanding in terms of the walking stamina required to reach them.

In addition to a description about each of the twelve sites and monuments I focus on, there is information on how to get there and what to expect in terms of terrain, interesting or quirky facts, recommendations on where to go for food and drink and suggestions about where else to visit in the vicinity.

Many thanks to Liz and Ed ffrench-Constant who have helped me with this project. They were my human companions on this adventure – taking many of the photos and helping with the planning. Big thanks to Daisy and Otto too. As the canine members of our team, they played an important part in testing out dog-friendly facilities, cafés and accommodation. We couldn't have done it without you!

Finally, big thanks to Anna Corbett, my editor at Tor Mark Press. She was the person who first mentioned the idea of a Secret Devon book – leading to many wonderful months of wanderings and musings on my part. As always, it's been a great pleasure to work with you and everyone else at Tor Mark.

Have fun exploring,

Sue

DREWSTEIGNTON

EX6 6QR

Centuries-old thatched cottages, an impressive central church and a famous pub that has no bar. Situated within glorious countryside above the Teign Gorge, historic Drewsteignton is a village well worth navigating through narrow lanes to access. It's small, peaceful and charming, in an unpretentious, time-stood-still sort of way. This is a place where total strangers are given a no-nonsense welcome (at least in my experience) and where trust is such that, when I asked if I could take a photo of a Daily Telegraph article about Mabel Mudge, her successor at The Drewe Arms pressed a book into my hands 'because it tells her story more accurately' and told me to 'post it back when you've finished with it'.

'Aunt Mabel', as she was fondly known, ran the pub from 1919 until she finally retired at the age of 99 in 1994. She and her husband, Ernest, had taken over the business from her brother-in-law, Alfred Mudge, who'd been landlord there for 26 years. Ernest died in 1951 and Mabel carried on, becoming the UK's longest-serving landlady and a well-deserved legend in her own lifetime. The pub, which was her home for the best part of a century, is now a Grade II listed building. Despite this little has changed – customers are still served drinks from three hatches in a room with long wooden benches and a cosy, very local feel.

Drewsteignton is one of the oldest parishes in Devon and, during the 12th century, a Norman named Drogo (Drew in English) was given the stewardship of Tainton. Hundreds of years later, self-made millionaire Julius Drewe decided Drogo was his ancestor and went on to buy the nearby estate. He commissioned architect Edward Lutyens to design a castle suited to the dynasty he claimed, which is perched high above the River Teign and is now owned by the National Trust. Castle Drogo is a strange, unmissable folly, that attracts thousands of visitors to its austere walls, beautiful gardens and incredible location.

Peter Randall-Page, *Granite Song 1991*, Dartmoor Granite © Paul Moody

Useful info...

- Sat Nav: EX6 6QR
- Suitable for dogs on a lead
- Accessible to everyone
- Limited parking in the village square and on the roadside
- Local post office sells a range of goods
- Any sort of footwear
- No public toilets

Time for Tea

The National Trust café at Castle Drogo (EX6 6PB) offers a good range of hot and cold snacks and light meals. Dogs aren't allowed at the tables. Alternatively, head for the picturesque Fingle Bridge Inn, right next to the river, where you and your canine companion can enjoy refreshments on the terrace or in the bar.

What Else?

One of the country's best sculptors, Peter Randall-Page, lives and works on the outskirts of Drewsteignton. One of his works, *Granite Song*, is permanently on display on a tiny island on the River Teign.

To find it, follow the Two Moors Way from Chagford along the river's west bank. When you come to a gate at the beginning of a wooded area, on your right you'll see the stone, which appears to be cut open revealing a seed in its middle.

Coming in the other direction, park at Dogmarsh Bridge, near the Mill End Hotel (TQ13 8JN) and follow the river towards Chagford. The amazing sculpture, which apparently had to be winched down by helicopter, will then be on your left.

What's Nearby?

• Castle Drogo (EX6 6PB) work started on this 20th century castle in 1911 and was finally completed in 1930, just a year before its creator, Julius Drewe, died. Sadly, his eldest son, Adrian, had been killed at Ypres, Belgium, in 1917, and there is a room in the superbly positioned castle that's devoted to his memory. Make sure you wander round the magnificent gardens and some of the estate trails. There are walks of various lengths providing wonderful views of Teign Gorge. Paid entry. www.nationaltrust.org. uk/castle-drogo

• Fingle Bridge (EX6 6PW) named after the stream that rises at Whiddon Down. This picturesque bridge, built in the early 1600s, is a popular beauty spot. Follow the riverside Fisherman's Path towards Chagford or, if you're feeling energetic, climb the Hunter's Path to Castle Drogo. Better still, do the circular walk that includes both. www. nationaltrust.org.uk/fingle-bridge

• Chagford (TQ13 8BN) originally built in the 1300s as a stannary town where tin was bought and sold, Chagford is picture-postcard pretty with a lovely square, historic buildings and a very relaxed, old-fashioned feel.

Fingle Bridge © Drewsteignton Parish Council

In a nutshell

The Drewsteignton area is full of interest and character, with plenty of amazing places to walk in the surrounding valleys. Everyone I met was very friendly (one landlord even lent my friends a dog bowl) and there's a strong sense of community.

STONE LANE GARDENS

TQ13 8JU

It's hard to imagine that what was once a poor growing five-acre field on the edge of Dartmoor National Park could be turned into a glorious garden that holds National Collection status for birch and alder trees. Yet that's precisely what modern-day plant hunter Kenneth Ashburner achieved. From 1971 onwards, he began transforming the land in front of his thatched cottage into a beautifully landscaped horticultural haven, full of unusual specimens collected from his travels across the world.

Nor is it just the woodland that enchants. Follow the paths as they meander around ponds, groves of trees, shade-loving plants and secret nooks to discover sculptures perfectly framed by their surroundings. There are fairies dangling from trees, huge birds, motionless deer and boxing hares — a magical juxtaposition of art and nature inspired by Kenneth's wife, June. Each year new works are contributed by local artists, creating a visitor experience that effortlessly blends adventure, myth and space for quiet reflection.

Sadly, Kenneth and June have both passed away, but their legacy continues. The garden is now run by a charity that oversees its continued development, conservation and care. Just two miles along narrow, winding lanes from Chagford, it's a memorable place for all ages to while away a couple of hours amidst gleaming tree barks, gently running streams and peaceful, unexpected glades.

Useful info...

- Sat Nav: TQ13 8JU
- The garden is open seven days a week, 365 days a year, from 10am to 6pm in the summer and 10am to dusk in the winter
- There is an admission charge, payable in an honesty box at the entrance
- Dogs on leads are welcome
- There is an on-site specialist tree nursery – visits by appointment only
- The garden is accessible to those with impaired mobility
- Visits are self-guided, but group tours can be arranged. Flat, robust footwear is advised
- Limited car parking is available
- There is a chemical toilet on-site
- There is no shop or café
- For more information, visit www.stonelanegardens.com

DID YOU KNOW?

Birch paper is very durable and has been used over many centuries worldwide for writing manuscripts. The wood also has a natural resonance that has made it a popular choice for making drums and speaker cabinets. In Celtic cultures, birch trees are said to symbolise growth, renewal, stability and adaptability, whilst in Gaelic folklore, they are associated with death and fairies.

Spinster's Rock (TQ13 8JX) Devon's best surviving example of a Neolithic burial chamber. Standing in a farmer's field (there were sheep in there when I visited), the ancient structure — three upright stones supporting a large horizontal slab — is an impressive sight. Originally surrounded by a number of other stones arranged in circles or rows and covered in earth to form a barrow. Legend has it that three spinsters somehow managed to erect it, by themselves, one morning before breakfast. Hardly likely, of course, but a good story that has given the dolmen its name.

Spinster's Rock

Time for Tea

The Sandy Park Inn (TQ13 8JW) is a delightful, thatched pub that offers a warm welcome and a selection of 'rustic food' during opening hours. It's dog-friendly and humans and canines alike will love the roaring fire and relaxed, friendly atmosphere. If you're looking for a scrumptious afternoon tea, the nearby Mill End Hotel (TQ13 8JN) offers a very special treat.

• Moretonhampstead Motor Museum (TQ13 8LG) home to over 130 historic vehicles, including machines from pre-1920s to the 1990s. Paid entry. Visit www.moretonmotormuseum.co.uk for details.

• Becky Falls (TQ13 9UG) a woodland park attraction that has a spectacular 70-foot high waterfall at its heart. There are some beautiful woodland walks in the area — clearly graded according to ability and family activities that include a zoo. Paid entry. Visit www.beckyfalls.com for details.

• Miniature Pony Centre (TQ13 8RG) plenty of animals, parkland walks and indoor and outdoor play areas — a place guaranteed to keep the whole family amused but dogs not permitted. Paid entry. Visit www.miniatureponycentre.com for details.

In a nutshell

Wandering around the gardens was a real delight — even during the winter. An unusual, beautiful place that's full of horticultural and artistic interest.

GRIMSPOUND

PL20 6TB

One of the joys of Dartmoor is the sense of timelessness you feel when surrounded by a landscape that's wild, untamed and relatively free from modern day influence and clutter. It's a feeling that you'll almost certainly get at Grimspound – a large, Bronze Age settlement high up on north-facing hills between Hameldown and Hookney Tor.

Clearly marked by what was once a nine-foot wide, circular wall and situated close to a small stream, known as Grim's Lake, Grimspound is about four acres in size. The area encloses the remains of 24 huts and the remnants of nine more outside the perimeter. It's thought the structures were once a mixture of dwellings and cattle pens – a farming community protecting itself from animal predators, rather than humans, in what would then have been dense forests below.

Look closely and you can still see where our ancestors would have cooked and warmed themselves by a fire. Their beds, positioned by the door, were granite slabs covered with heather and animal skins. Each building would have been constructed with paved floors and cone shaped roofs made from turf and thatch. Excavations have revealed porches, raised benches, cooking holes, charcoal, pottery and flint – physical reminders of lives lived when the weather is likely to have been warmer and drier than it is today and when the surrounding ground at Grimspound was probably more fertile.

To get to the site, park in the layby near Headland Warren Farm. You'll find a sign pointing uphill to the settlement, a short walk away.

Daisy & Otto exploring Grimspound

Useful info...

- Sat Nav: PL20 6TB
- Robust walking boots are recommended for the uneven ground
- Be careful of sheep when walking your dog
- The route is steep and unsuitable for those with impaired mobility
- There are no shops or toilets

— Time for Tea —

After an energising walk on the moor, the Warren House Inn (PL20 6TA) is the perfect place to cosy up to a fire that's been consistently burning since 1845! Visible from Grimspound (when it isn't foggy), the pub is famous both for its remoteness and its legends.

Several ghosts are said to haunt the premises at night – lending plenty of additional atmosphere. Perhaps you'll stumble across the landlord who shot himself at the bar in 1929, or the father of another landlord, whose corpse was said to have been salted and kept in a chest until the ground was sufficiently thawed to bury him!

The pub gets its electrical power from an on-site generator and water is gravity-fed from an underground stream. Gas for cooking comes from an LPG storage container, so there's a good menu and little chance of going hungry.

┌ DID YOU KNOW? ┐

A golden dagger, Dartmoor's richest archaelogical find, was found when a cairn on Hameldown ridge was excavated. Cut from a single piece of amber, its pommel was studded with hundreds of tiny gold pins. It isn't known whether there was any link with Grimspound just below, but the craftsmanship was superb and certainly an indication of great wealth and status. The find was made by a local dentist and antiquarian in 1872 and subsequently taken to Plymouth Museum for safe storage. Sadly, a wartime bombing raid in 1942 destroyed it – leaving only photos of the precious, and very significant, artefact.

Dartmoor is home to thousands of skylarks, making it a perfect place to see the small, mottled brown bird known for bursting into wonderful song as it rises vertically from the ground and hovers.

Skylarks nest in long grass and lay their eggs in the summer — they leave the moor in late August to spend the autumn and winter in lower-lying farmland. Watching them is apparently a good way of weather forecasting. When it's fine, they descend slowly but, when rain is likely, they drop quickly.

Skylarks are the second most numerous breeding bird on Dartmoor, with the meadow pipit claiming the top spot.

Skylark

enclosure below. It lies on the Two Moors Way.

• Birch Tor (SX686814) an easy walk from the nearby B3212 road and home to Vitifer Mine, which produced tin in significant quantities from 1852 until 1886. The miners who worked there had been sacked from other mining companies for minor offences and conditions were said to be especially tough.

• Challacombe stone rows (SX68988082) three impressive lines of 82 visible stones that were probably erected in the Bronze Age. Park on the B3212, just to the north of the Warren House Inn (PL20 6TA) and follow the miners' path towards Headland Warren. The triple row of stones is situated between Birch Tor and the summit of Challacombe Down.

• Hookney Tor (SX6990681317) to your left, as you face Grimspound from the road, it's well worth walking up to its cragged, granite top and looking down on the prehistoric circular

In a nutshell

You can let your imagination run wild visiting Grimspound. The walk from the road is invigorating, the views far-reaching and the prehistoric remains fascinating. A great place to stretch the mind as well as the legs.

WISTMAN'S WOOD

GRID REF: SX612774

Eerily beautiful in a strange, mystical way, Wistman's Wood is one of Dartmoor's unexpected treasures. Wild, daunting and terrifyingly bizarre, it appears as if out of nowhere in a moorland landscape that is otherwise windswept and bereft of much foliage. Entering it is a challenge because of the large, lichen-covered boulders strewn everywhere but clambering over them is the best way of truly appreciating this ancient woodland, with its stunted, pendunculate oak trees, thickly luxuriant mosses and still, magical feel.

Leaning against the huge stones that make it impossible for animals to graze, it's easy to see why few dare to enter Wistman's Wood after the sun goes down. The Druids performed pagan rituals here, ghosts are said to haunt the place and legend has it that it's also home to the Wisht Hounds – Satan's pack of black, demon dogs who, with fiery eyes and an insatiable blood lust, reputedly prey on the lost or unwary. During daylight hours adders are more of a worry, so be careful where you tread as you slither and slide on the rocks.

Wistman's Wood is likely to date back thousands of years to a time when Dartmoor was covered in forest. Climate change and farming have made vast areas treeless – creating a canopied enchantment that's a memorable anomaly.

To get there, head for the Two Bridges Hotel, cross the road to the cottage and the small car park opposite and follow the footpath signs. Pass Crockern Cottage and continue along the route, keeping the river to your left. After about a mile, you'll see Wistman's Wood rising from the riverbank.

Useful info...

- Grid Ref: SX612774
- Robust walking shoes or boots are recommended
- Take a waterproof coat in case the weather changes suddenly
- Be careful of sheep and other livestock when walking your dog
- There are some high stiles and big stones to negotiate
- The route is unsuitable for pushchairs and those with impaired mobility
- There are no shops or public toilets

DID YOU KNOW?

Wistman's Wood is made up of two main areas of woodland – the second that you come to being the largest. You'll find the Buller Stone here, just inside the perimeter. Three metres high and triangular, it bears the inscription: "By permission of HRH The Prince of Wales, Wentworth Buller, on Sept 16th 1868 cut down a tree near this spot. It measured 9in in diameter and appeared to be about 163 years old."

Time for Tea

The Two Bridges Hotel (Sat Nav: PL20 6SW) is likely to be your start and end point for visiting Wistman's Wood, so where better to relax and refresh after your bracing adventure? Dog-friendly, centuries-old and warmly welcoming, you can enjoy food and drink there all day long. Sit out on the terrace if the weather is fine or hunker down in front of an open fire in the lounge or bar when it's not. www.twobridges.co.uk

The road between Two Bridges and Postbridge is said to be haunted by a pair of severed hands that allegedly grab steering wheels, reins and handlebars, forcing cars, carts and bikes off the road. In June 1921, a doctor from Dartmoor Prison was riding his motorbike in the area, with his children in the sidecar, when he mysteriously lost control and was killed. Weeks later, an army captain reported being victim to a similar 'hairy hands' incident but, like the doctor's children, thankfully survived. Over the years, many others have claimed to have been terrified by the unlikely 'hands' apparition – a legendary evil menace that evokes cynicism and fear in equal measure.

What's Nearby?

• The Powder Mills and Powder Mills Pottery (PL20 6SP) on the road from Two Bridges to Postbridge, you'll see the old gunpowder mills on your left. Built in 1846, the factory supplied gunpowder to nearby mines. Part of these Grade II listed buildings now include the home, workplace and shop of potter Joss Hibbs.

• Postbridge (PL20 6TH) a small hamlet that boasts one of the finest medieval clapper bridges in the country, an excellent National Park Visitor Centre and a very good shop and post office. The bridge probably replaced stepping stones to make it easier for packhorses to cross the river.

• Bellever Forest (PL20 6TU) family-friendly, scenic and a great place to picnic by the East Dart River, Bellever is full of archaeological and wildlife interest.

Clapper Bridge, Postbridge

Bellever Forest

In a nutshell

Myths and legends abound on Dartmoor – and nowhere feels more spookily supernatural than Wistman's Wood and the surrounding area. A 'must' for anyone who enjoys an intriguing landscape and compelling, other-worldly tales.

BUCKLAND BEACON

PL20 6TA

Most of us know the story of Moses and the Ten Commandments – far fewer will be aware that Dartmoor boasts its own version. In fact, the Devon variant goes one better with 11 commandments painstakingly carved onto two granite slabs high up on Buckland Beacon.

Created in 1928, after a proposed new Book of Common Prayer was rejected by Parliament, the project was commissioned by local landowner and religious traditionalist William Whitley of Wellstor. Appalled by the prospect of having the original ten commandments reduced to two, he celebrated parliamentary victory by commissioning a local sculptor, W. A. Clement, to engrave the granite stones. Clement was instructed to carve the full list and then add an additional one from John, Chapter 13, Verse 34: 'A new commandment I give unto you. Love one another.'

The work was carried out from the 23rd July until the 31st August, during which time Mr. Carver reportedly laboured on-site for 9½ hours every day, whilst living in a cowshed, sleeping on wire netting and using a local stream for washing and drinking. He earned £50 for his efforts (more than £3000 now) and left an enduring legacy on a spectacular moorland landmark. The stones have been restored twice in recent years – firstly in 1995 and again in 2016.

┌─ D I D   Y O U   K N O W ? ─┐

Buckland Beacon is 382m high and enjoys magnificent, far reaching views. It's for those reasons that it's one of Dartmoor's fire beacon sites – nowadays used to celebrate milestone events like the millennium and royal jubilees. Thanks to a long coastline which made it vulnerable to attack, Devon has 89 beacon sites that are thought to date back to Roman times. When danger threatened, the fires were lit as both warning and signal.

William Whitley's grave in St Peter's Church graveyard

St Peter's Church

Widecombe-in-the-Moor

Useful info...

- Sat Nav: PL20 6TA (SX741743)
- To get to Buckland Beacon, park at Cold East Cross (Sat Nav: PL20 6TA) and take the southerly track towards the Beacon (OS Grid Ref: SX734731)
- The walk to Buckland Beacon is flat, level and relatively easy but unsuitable for wheelchairs
- Robust walking boots are recommended
- Be careful of sheep when walking your dog
- There are no shops or toilets

As well as being the man behind the commandments' stones on Buckland Beacon, William Whitley was also responsible for the unique clock at St Peter's Church in Buckland-in-the-Moor. Installed in 1930 as a gift, numbers on the face are replaced by letters spelling 'MY DEAR MOTHER', in memory of Mr Whitley's mother, who had died the previous year. It's a strange, touching and very compelling tribute. The church itself dates from around 1400 and boasts Tudor roof bosses and a remarkable rood screen. The thatched vestry outside is thought to be the only one of its kind still in use in England.

• Buckland-in-the-Moor (TQ13 7HN) a lovely little hamlet with a cluster of thatched cottages that overlooks the woodland of Holne Chase.

• Dartmeet (TQ13 7PT) the popular beauty spot where the east and west Dart tributaries meet in a steep, wooded valley. There's a large car park, a stone clapper bridge and plenty of space for picnics.

• River Dart Country Park (TQ13 7NP) set in 90 acres, the estate has a wide range of family activities to offer. From zip wires to canoeing and bike trails to climbing pods, outdoor fun is guaranteed. www.riverdart.co.uk

Dartmeet

Time for Tea

The Old Inn, Widecombe-in-the-Moor (Sat Nav: TQ13 7TA). There's plenty of atmosphere in this centuries-old pub standing at the heart of a charming, historic village. Resident ghost Harry is said to make his presence felt occasionally in the older parts, throwing things and weaving string around the kitchen equipment. Dog-friendly and offering a wide-range of menu options, the inn is a good place to relax, refresh and recharge. www.theoldinnwidecombe.com

In a nutshell

I loved the fact that someone was prepared to spend about six weeks working high up on a moorland beacon, carving 11 commandments onto stone, whilst sleeping rough in a local barn. Mr Carver's work is certainly worth the walk to see – as is its location.

WESTCOMBE BEACH

TQ7 4QE

Secluded, unspoilt and perfectly positioned between jagged rocks and steeply sloping hillsides, Westcombe Beach is a real gem. Getting to the beach demands a walk however you approach it, but any effort is rewarded with a sizeable sandy cove and dramatic seascape. There is no public road nearby and no facilities, making this a coastal treasure you're likely to enjoy in relative solitude.

To get to it, I walked from Kingston, a small village in the heart of South Devon's designated Area of Outstanding Natural Beauty (AONB). Kingston boasts charming thatched cottages and a 16th century inn, which was built to house the workers who constructed the church behind. From the inn, walk in the opposite direction to the church, then turn right at the junction. Go uphill, then turn left in front of a whitewashed cottage and onto an unmade track. Continue along the path as it wends its way beside a stream and some ponds, eventually bearing right. When you reach a fork that gives you the option to turn left uphill, follow the sign that directs you over a stile and towards Westcombe Beach. The route opens up into a steep-sided valley with Hoist Point to your right and the sea ahead.

Having reached the sand and explored the cove (look out for a view of Burgh Island between the rocks to your left), you can go back the way you came. Alternatively, if you can muster up enough energy, take a climb up the headland which is owned by the National Trust, then follow the South West Coast Path to Fernycombe Point before turning back inland. When you reach the fork after the signpost turn left up the field. The path eventually becomes tarmacked. Carry on until you get to a T-junction, where you turn right back to the village.

Westcombe Beach

Useful info...

- Sat Nav (Kingston village): TQ7 4QE
- There is parking at the local pub, or park sensitively on the side of the road
- Good walking shoes and boots are recommended
- If you've got your dog with you, be aware there may be ducks in the stream and ponds
- The track can be very muddy and there are some steep slopes
- There are a couple of stiles, making the route difficult for those with impaired mobility
- The beach is dog-friendly all year round
- If you choose the South West Coast Path route, be careful with your dog and children near cliff edges
- There is no shop or public toilets in Kingston

DID YOU KNOW?

The church of St James the Less in Kingston originates from the 14th century but, although at that time local people could be christened and married, it was many years before burials were permitted. Coffins were carried to the churchyard at Ermington, nearly five miles away, until parishioners' complaints finally achieved approval to bury their dead in the village from the Pope in February 1402. The church originally had a peal of four bells, the oldest of which dates from 1430. In 1979, the bells were retuned and two new ones added. Considered an important part of Kingston life, they are rung to mark celebrations and tolled at funerals.

The Dolphin Inn

Another walk or short drive from Kingston takes you to Wonwell Beach on the Erme Estuary. At low tide, there is a large expanse of sand to enjoy and the scenery is spectacular. Dogs are permitted all year round but, if you are planning to take the car, be aware that parking is very limited, especially during the summer. Wonwell has been used as a location for TV series and the 1978 film, *International Velvet*. The estuary is regularly visited by a range of birds including egrets, curlew, oystercatchers, shelduck and kingfishers.

Kingfisher

Time for Tea

No visit to Kingston would be complete without a visit to The Dolphin Inn. Dating from the 16th century, it has plenty of character and charm with beamed ceilings, an open fire and excellent food. Very dog-friendly and welcoming, there are gardens to sit in during warmer weather and for those looking for an accommodation base, some guest rooms. Having stayed there myself, I can particularly recommend the breakfasts. www.dolphininnkingston.co.uk

• Modbury (PL21 0QR) a small and very picturesque market town, just three miles from Kingston. Famous for being the first community in Britain to ban plastic bags, the pretty streets are full of independent shops, pubs and cafés.

• Ringmore (TQ7 4HL) a delightfully quaint village with the Journey's End Inn at its heart. Dating from the 13th century and once allegedly a smugglers' haunt, the hostelry inspired R.C. Sherriff's 1920s play of the same name – written whilst the playwright was staying there.

• Kingsbridge Cookworthy Museum (TQ7 1AW) housed in the town's old grammar school, the museum tells the story of Kingsbridge and the South Hams through artefacts and old photographs. For opening hours and admission charges, visit www.kingsbridgemuseum.org.uk

In a nutshell

The walk and discovery of Westcombe Beach felt truly special. Unspoilt nature on a grand scale and an energising experience that Daisy, my dog, thoroughly enjoyed too.

SECRET DEVON

03
GRIMSPOUND
PAGE 15

04
WISTMAN'S WOOD
PAGE 19

Sourton

Gunnislake

*Tamar Valley
Area of Outstanding
Natural Beauty*

Woolwell

Saltash

PLYMOUTH

06
WESTCOMBE BEACH
PAGE 27

07
BURGH ISLAND
PAGE 33

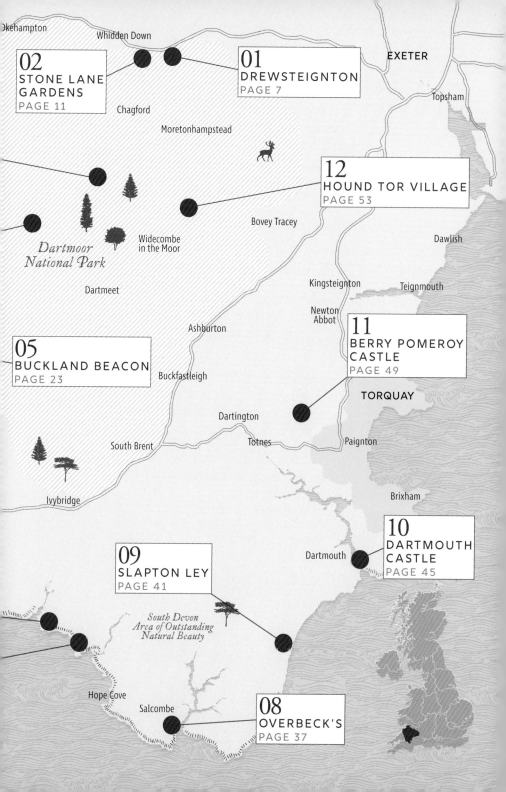

Okehampton

Whidden Down

02
STONE LANE
GARDENS
PAGE 11

Chagford

Moretonhampstead

01
DREWSTEIGNTON
PAGE 7

EXETER

Topsham

12
HOUND TOR VILLAGE
PAGE 53

Bovey Tracey

Dawlish

*Dartmoor
National Park*

Widecombe
in the Moor

Dartmeet

Kingsteignton

Teignmouth

Newton
Abbot

Ashburton

05
BUCKLAND BEACON
PAGE 23

Buckfastleigh

11
BERRY POMEROY
CASTLE
PAGE 49

TORQUAY

Dartington

South Brent

Totnes

Paignton

Ivybridge

Brixham

10
DARTMOUTH
CASTLE
PAGE 45

09
SLAPTON LEY
PAGE 41

Dartmouth

*South Devon
Area of Outstanding
Natural Beauty*

Hope Cove

Salcombe

08
OVERBECK'S
PAGE 37

BURGH ISLAND
TQ7 4BG

Cut off from the mainland twice a day when the tide comes in, Burgh Island is, quite literally, a place apart. Twenty-six acres of wind-blown terrain, perilous cliff drops and secluded coves combine to make it a beguiling curiosity. Thanks to the Art Deco hotel that was built there in 1929, it continues to attract the rich and very famous.

Agatha Christie wrote two of her books on the island and a three-day stay for Noel Coward turned into three weeks. Small it may be, but what is lacking in terms of space is more than made up for by an intensity of experience that ebbs and flows with the sea. There are few trees and little natural shelter. Exposed to the elements, Burgh Island – for all its exclusivity – is wild, untamed and dramatic.

Originally called St Michael's Island, it's thought a monastery once stood where the hotel now presides. There was also a chapel on the summit, which later became a huer's hut for lookouts who would let local fishermen know when shoals of pilchards were spotted. That then became an observation post in World War Two – a perfect vantage point for any sign of German invasion.

When the tide is out, you can walk across the beach from Bigbury-on-Sea to Burgh Island. When the water swirls around (worth waiting for), a sea tractor – the only one of its kind in the world – provides a unique and memorable form of transport.

Useful info...

- Sat Nav: TQ7 4BG
- Walking shoes are recommended for exploring the island
- Dogs are welcome but it's advisable to keep them on leads
- There's a pay and display car park in Bigbury-on-Sea
- There are public toilets and shops in Bigbury
- Those with impaired mobility can access the island but might find the climb to its summit a challenge

The Pilchard Inn

Time for Tea

The island's Pilchard Inn was first established in 1396. Legend has it that there was once a tunnel running from a cave on the beach, which smuggler, Tom Crocker, used to haul booty to the pub where it was stored. Sitting with a glass of chilled white wine and a crab baguette within the building's thick, ancient walls, it's not hard to imagine what might have gone on in the past. Owned by the hotel, the inn offers an all-day menu and is the perfect place to watch the tide roll in.

Burgh Island Hotel

What Else?

The beach at Bigbury-on-Sea is ideal for families in search of sun, sea, sand and rockpools during the warmer months. The water is relatively safe and monitored by lifeguards and there are local hire facilities for those wanting to take part in popular sports, like bodyboarding, surfing, kitesurfing and windsurfing. Designated areas are accessible to dogs all year round and there's a good, local café that is open all day. Once a tiny fishing hamlet, the village has grown to become a seaside destination in its own right – with iconic Burgh Island just 270 yards offshore.

What's Nearby?

• Aveton Gifford (TQ7 4LL) situated three miles inland at the head of the Avon estuary, the village has a centuries-old history (its manor was listed in the Domesday Book) and is surrounded by beautiful, unspoilt countryside. Situated next to a tranquil stream, the Fisherman's Rest pub enjoys an excellent reputation for 'good honest food' at reasonable prices. www.thefishermansrest. co.uk

• Ringmore to Ayrmer Cove walk is a wonderful way to appreciate the beauty of the Ringmore Valley and some fabulous views across to Burgh Island. Start from the National Trust car park (TQ7 4HR) and follow the sign for Ayrmer Cove. Three miles in length and moderate in terms of terrain, the

route is circular. www.nationaltrust.org.uk/ringmore-and-kingston/trails/ringmore-to-ayrmer-cove-walk

• Thurlestone (TQ7 3PA) the village takes its name from the Thurlestone Rock, an arch-shaped rock formation in Thurlestone Bay. Thurlestone Beach is sheltered and generally very peaceful, with shallow waters for children to play in. Lifeguards are on duty over the summer. www.visitsouthdevon.co.uk/things-to-do/thurlestone-beach-p1200703

Aveton Gifford

In a nutshell

Burgh Island is compelling. Devon's answer to St Michael's Mount – but with a hut, rather than a castle, on its peak and a chic hotel on its mainland-facing flank. I love its sense of mystery, seascape drama and secret spaces. Little wonder it has proved such an inspiration for famous creative geniuses.

OVERBECK'S

TQ8 8LW

Described by the National Trust as a 'hidden paradise of sub-tropical gardens', Overbeck's is a horticultural treasure trove. Perched high above Salcombe, the views over the estuary and coast are simply breathtaking. Add in rare and exotic plant collections from around the world, spread over seven acres of terraced grounds accessed via a series of meandering pathways, and wonder is guaranteed.

I visited in early spring when the magnificent *Magnolia campbellii* 'Overbecks' was in full, dazzling splendour. Planted in 1901, it's a vision of deep rose-pink flowers that's set against a panorama of sea, cliffs and a vast expanse of uninterrupted sky. In summer, it's the Japanese Wisteria and the Dierama (Angels Fishing Rods) that flourish whilst, in the autumn, the hardy Japanese banana comes into its own, together with the red-splashed foliage of the *Musa Sikkimensis* and the 'Assam Orange'.

The property's last private owner, research chemist Otto Overbeck, was an accomplished linguist, artist and inventor. His greatest commercial success was the 'electrical rejuvenator' that he patented in the 1920s – claiming it could defy the ageing process. The device was successfully marketed worldwide, and the profits allowed Overbeck to buy this Salcombe home in 1928. After his death in 1937, it was bequeathed to the National Trust.

The house, which was a hospital during the war and subsequently a youth hostel, is now a museum. Full of the many objects Otto collected during his travels, pride of place is understandably given to his famous rejuvenator. Did it work? He obviously thought so – announcing that, aged 64, he felt like a man of 30. Presumably many others were convinced too, enabling Overbeck to end his days in a stunning location that enjoys its own Mediterranean micro-climate.

Magnolia campbellii

Saltcombe Beach

Useful info...

- Sat Nav: TQ8 8LW
- There is a small car park with a limited number of spaces. There is also some parking available on nearby roads
- Be prepared for some fairly steep uphill walking to reach Overbeck's
- Sturdy flat footwear is recommended
- Only assistance dogs are allowed into the house and gardens
- There is a tearoom and a shop selling gifts, plants and local produce
- There are toilet facilities
- There are gravel paths, which are not accessible to wheelchairs
- For more information, visit www.nationaltrust.org.uk/overbecks

---

DID YOU KNOW?

Otto Overbeck probably invented marmite. Whilst working in a brewery in Grimsby, he discovered that a waste product from the brewing process was in fact a nutritious food. He called it 'carnos', which is Greek for meat, formed a company to produce it and took out a patent. The latter was left to expire, and almost as soon as it did, Marmite – virtually identical to carnos – was marketed commercially. A rather more enduring success story than the rejuvenator.

Time for Tea

It has to be the on-site tearoom. If the weather is mild, the terrace is a perfect place to eat and drink whilst enjoying spectacular views. If it isn't, you can retreat to the Edwardian splendour of the house and indulge in a cream tea or other light meals and refreshments. www.nationaltrust.org.uk/overbecks/features/eating-and-shopping-at-overbecks

View of Salcombe town

If you park at North Sands car park (TQ8 8JQ), you can walk to Overbeck's via the South West Coast Path. The route takes you via Collaton Wood, South Sands beach and Splatcove Point. After visiting Overbeck's, you can carry on to Sharp Tor and look over Starehole Bay. Continue on, until you reach Bolt Head to make the most of the amazing sea and landscape. From there, head north west along the coast path towards Middle Soar where you turn right inland. Turn right into Tor Woods, before heading back towards the car park. The walk is about five miles in length, with some steep stretches.

• Salcombe a watersports haven and picturesque town that offers plenty in the way of upmarket retail therapy. Originally a community that survived on what it could harvest from the sea, it has evolved into an exclusive holiday resort that still earns its income largely from the water and the leisure industry its unrivalled coastal position has spawned. www.salcombeinformation.co.uk

• Salcombe Maritime Museum (TQ8 8DE) full of models of ships, paintings, photographs and artefacts, the museum tells the story of Salcombe's maritime origins. A young sailor's corner will keep the children amused too. www.salcombemuseum.org.uk

What's Nearby?

• South Devon Chilli Farm (TQ7 4DX) from hobby to very successful business, this is the place to visit for all things chilli – from sauces and chutneys to jellies and chocolate. Open all year round and with a farm shop, café, nursery and play area, there's plenty to see, do and taste. www.southdevonchillifarm. co.uk

In a nutshell

I'm not particularly green-fingered, but Overbeck's combination of lush garden, interesting house and amazing location definitely delivered the wow factor. You have to properly explore to unravel its secret spaces, an adventure I highly recommend.

09

SLAPTON LEY

TQ7 2QN

Slapton Ley isn't just a nature reserve — it's a National Nature Reserve and designated Site of Special Scientific Interest. The largest freshwater lake in the Westcountry, it's 1.5 miles long and covers more than 490 acres of natural woodland, marshes and reedbed habitat — making it a haven for some rare and very special wildlife.

The ley is managed by the Field Studies Council and leased from the Whitley Wildlife Conservation Trust. It is separated from the sea and beach by a shingle ridge which, during the summer, is adorned by wildflowers like the yellow horned-poppy and Vipers Bugloss. The ley is a bird lover's paradise, where the Cetti's warbler can be heard and occasionally seen all year round. Bitterns and great crested grebes make regular appearances, and you can watch them from the bird hides that look out over the reeds.

Lucky observers might also see badgers, dormice, otters and bats in amongst the 250 species of lichen and 2000 species of fungi — 29 of which are said to be new to science.

A circular trail runs through the reserve that can take you as far as Slapton village if you're feeling energetic (the round route is about three miles). Alternatively, you might just want to amble a little way then sit on a bench and simply watch the wonders of nature around you — an experience I thoroughly recommend as a welcome antidote to the hustle and bustle of life.

Slapton Sands was the scene of Exercise Tiger, an important rehearsal for the D-Day landings that sadly turned into an horrific World War Two tragedy on the night of 27th April 1944. Local residents had been evacuated the previous year so that the long, sloping shingle beach could be used by thousands of predominantly American troops for the invasion practice. Unbeknown to the allied soldiers taking part, nine German E-boats were in the area and, when they detected the American landing craft, torpedoed three of them. A catastrophic mix-up in allied communications and the use of live fire from the shore rather than dummy bullets resulted in an official death toll at sea and on land of 749 men. That number could well be significantly higher but the exercise, for obvious wartime reasons, was shrouded in secrecy for the next three decades. What is certain is that the Americans taking part suffered fewer casualties on D-Day itself, and many operational lessons were learnt.

Slapton Sands Monument

Useful info...

- Sat Nav: TQ7 2QN
- There are car parks next to Slapton Sands beach (pay and display) and very limited off-road parking
- The trail is well-marked and level, but can become slippery and muddy
- There are public toilets in the Torcross and Memorial car parks
- Slapton Village Community Shop is at the end of Slapton's village hall car park, near the Slapton Ley Field Centre
- Dogs should be kept on leads to avoid disturbing the wildlife in the reserve
- Access to some parts of the trail might prove difficult for those with impaired mobility and pushchairs
- Robust footwear for walking is recommended and wellies would be a good idea if it is raining
- For more information, visit www.slnnr.org.uk

What Else?

Walking along the South West Coast Path, towards Start Point, will bring you to Hallsands, the village that famously fell into the sea on 26th January 1917. First established around 1600 as a fishing community, by 1891 Hallsands comprised of 37 houses and a pub. Dredging along the coastline to expand Keyham dockyard, near Plymouth, eroded the protective shingle. Although the work was stopped when the villagers protested, a violent storm breached their defences and all but one of the buildings succumbed to the sea. Thankfully, everyone survived.

What's Nearby?

• Start Point Lighthouse Visitor Centre (TQ7 2ET) owned by Trinity House, you can take a guided tour of the Grade II listed landmark during the summer months. Built in 1836 and modernised in 2019, the lighthouse still has an important role to play in alerting shipping to hazards posed by the Devon coast. www.trinityhouse.co.uk/lighthouses-and-lightvessels/start-point-lighthouse

• Beesands Beach (TQ7 2EH) the mile-long shingle sands are backed by the village green and a large freshwater lake known as Widdicombe Ley – another great place for spotting birds. There's a free car park close to the beach, which is popular for those wanting to surf and sail. www.thebeachguide.co.uk/south-west-england/devon/beesands.htm

• Exercise Tiger Memorial (TQ7 2TQ) first established in 1984, by the son of one of the many hundreds of men who died during the D-Day training operation, this is a must see stop for anyone interested in Slapton Sands and its history. Situated on the edge of Torcross village, a Sherman tank stands sentinel. The area is dedicated to those who lost their lives in a tragedy that nonetheless paved the way for subsequent allied invasion success, and the beginning of the end of the war.

Time for Tea

The Tower Inn in Slapton village might be tucked away but you can't miss the 14th century tower standing right next to it. The inn was built in 1347 – originally as cottages for the workmen building the adjacent ecclesiastical college. Old and full of character, it offers a sheltered walled garden during the summer and a roaring log fire in the winter as the setting for very good food and drink. www.thetowerinn.com

In a nutshell

Slapton Ley and its surrounding area are packed full of things to see and do. Whether you're walking, wildlife-gazing, beaching or finding out more about the past, there's plenty to engage and fascinate in this captivating part of the South Devon coast.

DARTMOUTH CASTLE

TQ6 0JN

Strategically positioned at the mouth of the River Dart, 14th century Dartmouth Castle is a historical delight. Managed by English Heritage and comprising a complex of fortifications (together with a church), there's plenty to wonder at – including a well-preserved, four-storey gun tower, a castle lighthouse and panoramic sea and estuary views.

First built in 1388 by successful merchant, privateer and shipowner John Hawley – who was first elected Mayor of Dartmouth at the age of 24 and is said to be the inspiration for Chaucer's flamboyant 'Shipman' in the *Canterbury Tales* – Dartmouth Castle has guarded its town for more than 600 years. The castle saw its first serious action during the English Civil War, when it was initially used to defend the Parliamentary cause. It was then taken by the Royalists who occupied it for over two years, until a two-day Parliamentary siege returned it to the opposition. Ensuing war with France over the next century ensured its retention as a defensive necessity and, after many years of peace in the 19th century, it was again brought back into service during both the First and Second World War.

As a visitor, you can explore the passageways, see the guardrooms and climb the battlements. Of particular interest is a feat of medieval engineering – a great iron chain that could at one time be deployed from the gun tower. It spanned the 250m opening of the Dart estuary and stopped enemy ships mid-river, so that guns could fire on the stranded vessels. The chain is no longer there but a creative animation shows how it would have worked.

Useful info...

- Sat Nav: TQ6 0JN
- There is a pay and display car park 12 metres from the entrance. There is also free parking on the access road
- You'll be climbing steps and walking on uneven surfaces so appropriate footwear is recommended
- Facilities include a tearoom, shop, picnic area and toilets
- Dogs on leads are welcome
- As an historical site, access is limited for those with impaired mobility
- For more information on opening hours and admission costs, visit www.english-heritage.org.uk/visit/places/dartmouth-castle

River Dart

Time for tea

There are plenty of options, including a good selection of hot and cold refreshments in the Dartmouth Castle tearoom. Boasting stunning river views, it's a lovely place to take a break from delving into local history with a cream tea, sandwich or light meal. You could also bring your own snacks and enjoy them on one of the site's picnic benches.

Dartmouth is a charming, historic town – full of narrow streets (beware when driving through or trying to park). Its quaint houses and variety of interesting shops and businesses are in a buzzing main street (especially during summer). The river is a constant source of distraction with a range of craft plying its beautiful waters. On the opposite side you'll find Kingswear – a small, steeply sloped village with colourful terraced houses, a more tranquil feel and access to some excellent (though strenuous) coastal walks. You can explore it by taking one of the regular ferry services that operate from Dartmouth.

• Dartmouth Museum (TQ6 9PZ) housed in a timber-framed old merchant's house and built around 1640, it's a treasure chest of artefacts, model ships, paintings and photos that tell the story of the town in fascinating detail. Hands-on exhibits make it appealing for younger members of the family too. www.devonmuseums.net/Dartmouth-Museum/Devon-Museums

• Bayard's Cove Fort (TQ6 9AX) only reached by foot, managed by English Heritage and built between 1522 and 1536, this Tudor fortification contained heavy guns to protect the town from attack. Picturesque and free to enter, it's another must-see piece of the Dartmouth historical jigsaw.

• Greenway house and garden (TQ5 0ES) the much-loved holiday home of famous crime writer Agatha Christie, this National Trust property is well worth the short ferry journey across the water to Kingswear. Famed as a 'Camellia Garden of Excellence' (one of only seven in the UK) and with a house full of objects collected by the family, you don't need to be a sleuth to discover Greenway's many secret delights. www.nationaltrust.org.uk/greenway

In a nutshell

Dartmouth may be well-known as a tourism destination, but take the time to find out more about its fascinating past. Dartmouth Castle is a real gem – not just for the historian but for anyone who appreciates breathtaking vistas and a very calming sense of timelessness.

BERRY POMEROY CASTLE

TQ9 6LJ

Berry Pomeroy Castle is one of those places you're unlikely to forget. Set amidst deep woods in Gatcombe Valley, it's an impressive ruin – not just of a 15th century castle but of a grand, Elizabethan mansion too. The combination is unusual, providing plenty to occupy anyone interested in history. There is something more though. Something that can best be described as a feeling that, whilst the inhabitants are long dead and gone, they have not quite departed.

I visited on a morning, when mist swirled over the ramparts and the many sightless windows yawned over a darkened courtyard, not yet lit by the promised sun. It was an eerie sight and one totally in keeping with Berry Pomeroy's long-held reputation as one of the most haunted landmarks in Britain. Ghost stories abound here and it's hard not to be spooked when wandering its passageways, peering round corners and descending stairs into dark, long-abandoned rooms. I didn't see Lady Margaret, who was allegedly locked up by her jealous sister and eventually starved to death, or the Blue Lady, whose incestuous relationship with her father led to the birth of a baby whom she is then said to have murdered, but it wasn't hard to imagine such apparitions occurring.

Originally built by the Pomeroy family as a place of greater safety than their nearby manor house during the Wars of the Roses, Berry Pomeroy started out as a fortified castle with towers, gun ports, battlements and a dry moat to deter attackers. In 1547, the Pomeroys sold to King Edward VI's uncle, Edward Seymour, Lord Protector Somerset, who had a modest Elizabethan house constructed within the medieval walls. The eldest brother of Jane Seymour (Henry VIII's third wife who died in childbirth), Edward, was accused of treason and beheaded just three years after taking on his Devon property. Further generations of the Seymour family continued to develop it on an immense scale but, in 1611, work came to an abrupt halt when the money ran out. By 1697, Berry Pomeroy was a ruin and has remained so ever since.

Useful info...

- Sat Nav: TQ9 6LJ
- There is a car park at the entrance to the castle
- Berry Pomeroy is still owned by the Duke of Somerset but managed by English Heritage
- There are toilets and an English Heritage shop on-site
- Sensible footwear for walking on uneven ground and climbing steep steps is recommended
- Only the grounds, shops and ground floor of the site are accessible to disabled visitors
- Dogs on leads are welcome
- For further information on admission charges and opening hours, visit www.english-heritage.org.uk/visit/places/berry-pomeroy-castle

Proud to have been welcoming guests since 1320, the Cott Inn, Dartington (TQ9 6HE) is one of the oldest, thatched hostelries in the country. With an excellent reputation for accommodation, food and all-round loveliness, it positively oozes character and charm. www.cottinn.co.uk

---

DID YOU KNOW?

Devon was the most lawless area in the south of England during the 15th century, thanks to warring feuds between land-owning families. In the 1450s it became even worse with the rift between the powerful houses of Lancaster and York. The Pomeroys were on the Yorkist side, whilst the Earl of Devon and his son, Thomas Courtenay, were on the other. The conflict resulted in the Pomeroys being violently evicted from their manor house, in Berry Pomeroy village, and deciding to build a castle on land they owned in the nearby area that was wooded, remote and more easily defended.

Once you've had a good look around the castle, take the time to get a wider perspective with a walk down through woods and a field to Castle Mill Farm, where you turn right to join the John Musgrave Heritage Trail – in its entirety, 35 miles long. Follow the road alongside the river and eventually a lake, before turning right up a steep, wooded path that takes you back to the castle. Look out for the Wishing Tree next to the car park at the top. It's a large beech tree that's said to grant any wish if you walk backwards around it three times. Probably not a good idea to try, though, given the uneven ground and the tree's huge roots.

What's Nearby?

• Berry Pomeroy Church (TQ9 6LQ) situated right next to the Pomeroys' original (and still inhabited) manor house, which they abandoned in favour of living in a more easily-defended castle, the church dates from the 11th century and enjoys lovely views of the surrounding countryside. Don't miss seeing the Seymour chapel, with its memorial to Lord Edward Seymour (son of the Protector), his son (another Edward) and his wife Elizabeth Champernowne. All are lying on their side, with their heads propped on their hands.

• Totnes Castle (TQ9 5NU) managed by English Heritage, the classic motte and bailey castle is within easy walking distance of the historic market town. www.english-heritage.org.uk/visit/places/totnes-castle

• Dartington Hall (TQ9 6EL) a 1200-acre estate that includes beautiful gardens, a magnificent deer park, miles of walks and an excellent events programme. www.dartington.org

Dartington Hall

In a nutshell

I've always wanted to visit Berry Pomeroy, but the reality was even better than imagined. You wouldn't expect to find ruins of such magnitude in a deep wood, high above the valley, yet that was the point of its construction. Romantic, hidden and perhaps, deceptively peaceful, the castle represents a past that many say has never truly died.

BERRY POMEROY CASTLE

HOUND TOR
VILLAGE
TQ13 9XG

Hound Tor is one of Dartmoor's better-known landmarks, but walk beyond the craggy outcrop, down the valley to the south east and you'll discover the remains of 11 stone buildings. With virtually no tree cover, it's a bleak, savage landscape, that's open to the elements. Hardly an ideal location for a village these days yet, in Medieval times, there's evidence to suggest it was once a thriving farming community.

The settlement is comprised of four longhouses, each with two entrances and a passage that divided people from their animals. You can see the drainage channel that marks where the livestock would have been kept – a practical arrangement, since cows generate heat and sharing a building with them would have been snug, if a little smelly. The largest house, which had two gardens, lies slightly apart within the complex – possibly denoting the home of a wealthier individual. Two other smaller dwellings nearby would probably once have homed dependents or labourers and a range of barns would have been used to dry the corn and oats grown on the land.

When inhabited, the weather was almost certainly much milder than it is today – becoming increasingly cold and wet during the 13th and 14th centuries. That would have made growing crops on the moor much harder – a contributing factor, perhaps, to the village being abandoned. There's some debate about when that might have happened, but the small community is unlikely to have escaped the impact of the Black Death, when it struck Devon in 1348. Around a third of the county's population succumbed to the merciless contagion, dying a horrible death that wiped out entire families. Those who survived might well have battled on in an environment that was becoming harsher for a while but, ultimately, everyone left.

Useful info...

- Sat Nav: TQ13 9XG
- There's a car park at the base of Hound Tor, about half a mile away from the village
- Sturdy, waterproof footwear is recommended
- It's an uphill climb from the car park to the tor and you'll then follow a rough track down to the settlement
- The terrain is unsuitable for those with impaired mobility
- Keep your dog under control as sheep and livestock roam the area
- There's often a mobile café selling hot and cold snacks in the car park
- There are no toilets

Time for Tea

The mobile catering van at Hound Tor – The Hound of the Basket Meals – is an obvious and very popular option. Serving a range of filled rolls, bacon baps, burgers and snacks, it will definitely keep the hunger pangs at bay. For a wider range of choices in traditional character cottage-style, try The Gateway Tea Room and Café in Moretonhampstead (TQ13 8PE). www.thegatewaytearoom.com

54

It has to be Hound Tor itself, two unmissable stacks of impressive rocks, with a gap, or 'avenue', between them, that's said to be haunted by a black dog and other ghosts. Sir Arthur Conan Doyle's famous Sherlock Holmes novel, *The Hound of the Baskervilles*, was apparently inspired by the landmark and it's not hard to see why. Sinister in certain lights and swirling in legend, it's the perfect setting for a tale of supernatural canine skullduggery.

What's Nearby?

• Jay's Grave (50.60509°N 3.79269°W) from Hound Tor car park, take the left fork and follow the minor road for about a mile. Kitty Jay was an orphan who was born in 1790 and grew up in a local poor house before finding work at Canna Farm near Manaton. Life was hard, but she fell for the farmer's son and became pregnant. Appalled, her lover's parents threw her out and, with her reputation ruined, she hanged herself in a barn. As she committed suicide she couldn't be buried in sacred ground, so a grave was dug at a crossroads. Legend has it that her ghost haunts the spot. Even more bizarrely, fresh flowers are placed on her final resting place every day – and no-one knows by whom.

• Bowerman's Nose (SX742805) a strange-looking column of rocks, close to Manaton, that looks uncannily like a man. Legend has it, of course, that it was once a man – Bowerman, a tall, powerful hunter who was generally very well-liked, except by the local witches. When his pack of hounds accidentally ran through one of their gatherings, causing chaos, the hags got their revenge by luring him into a trap and turning him to stone.

• Haytor (TQ13 9XT) possibly Dartmoor's most popular tor, thanks to its proximity to the road, where you can find large car parks and the handy Dartmoor National Park Visitor Centre. The two massive granite outcrops are pretty impressive too.

In a nutshell

No visit to the moor is complete without a visit to Hound Tor, but I found the deserted medieval village, beyond those haunting rocks, especially memorable. People lived there - probably for centuries - until a combination of climate change and hideous disease drove them from their homes. A monument to the past that's powerfully evocative.